Implementing Service Quality based on ISO/IEC 20000

A Management Guide

Implementing Service Quality based on ISO/IEC 20000

A Management Guide

Third edition

MICHAEL KUNAS

IT Governance Publishing

Every possible effort has been made to ensure that the information contained in this book is accurate at the time of going to press, and the publisher and the author cannot accept responsibility for any errors or omissions, however caused. Any opinions expressed in this book are those of the author, not the publisher. Websites identified are for reference only, not endorsement, and any website visits are always at the reader's own risk. No responsibility for loss or damage occasioned to any person acting, or refraining from action, as a result of the material in this publication can be accepted by the publisher or the author.

ITIL® is a registered trade mark of the Cabinet Office.

Apart from any fair dealing for the purposes of research or private study, or criticism or review, as permitted under the Copyright, Designs and Patents Act 1988, this publication may only be reproduced, stored or transmitted, in any form, or by any means, with the prior permission in writing of the publisher or, in the case of reprographic reproduction, in accordance with the terms of licences issued by the Copyright Licensing Agency. Enquiries concerning reproduction outside those terms should be sent to the publisher at the following address:

IT Governance Publishing
IT Governance Limited
Unit 3, Clive Court
Bartholomew's Walk
Cambridgeshire Business Park
Ely
Cambridgeshire
CB7 4EA
United Kingdom

www.itgovernance.co.uk

© Michael Kunas 2011, 2012
The author has asserted the rights of the author under the Copyright, Designs and Patents Act, 1988, to be identified as the author of this work.

First published in the United Kingdom in 2011
by IT Governance Publishing (978-1-84928-192-8).

Second edition 2012 (978-1-84928-402-8)

Third edition 2012 (978-1-84928-442-4)

FOREWORD

2011-12 will be an important time for IT service management, and especially for ISO/IEC 20000, for various reasons. First of all, the new versions of ISO/IEC 20000-1:2011 and ISO/IEC 20000-2:2012 are available.

Secondly, we have an increase of RFPs from the US government, which makes ISO/IEC 20000 an obligation for government tenders.

Recently, the US Air Force required an ISO/IEC 20000 certificate from sourcing providers for their Enterprise Integration and Services Management (EISM) system.

The RFP required:

'The prime contractor shall provide proof of certification (copy of certificate) of ISO/IEC 20000. This certification must be held at the prime offeror's organisational level performing the contract.'

It further says: 'As a minimum, the prime contractor shall be certified ISO/IEC 20000 for the entire performance period of the contract, inclusive of options'.

Last, but not least, more RFPs which require ISO/IEC 20000 certification are on the way: US Department of Defense, NIST and US Veterans' Affairs have indicated a preference for ISO/IEC 20000 certificates for upcoming help desk proposals.

PREFACE

This management guide is the result of some coincidences.

I was initially looking for a Spanish version of Alan Calder's management guide on ISO/IEC 27000. Having made contact with Alan Calder, discussions followed and I was given the opportunity to write this management guide for the ISO/IEC 20000 Standard.

The other side of the story is as follows:

Plato said there are four things a man should do in his life:

1. That he should plant a tree.

2. That he should write a book.

3. That he should get a child.

4. That he should build a house.

One, three and four are already done, so here goes the book!

ABOUT THE AUTHOR

Michael Kunas is an ISO/IEC 20000 Lead Auditor and ITSM Consultant, living and working with his wife and son in sunny Madrid (Spain). He has over 15 years' experience in all areas of computer science.

After finishing his Masters in Computer Science in Germany, he moved to England for a while, where he co-worked on a book about Maths software. Shortly afterwards, he fell for the Spanish sun! In his spare time, he enjoys reading science fiction books.

ACKNOWLEDGEMENTS

A number of people have helped make this book possible. This includes Alan Calder, who provided the opportunity and encouragement to write this management guide.

Dr Suzanne D. Van Hove (Founder and CEO of SED-IT) and Marc Taillefer (past Secretary of the international Working Group writing the ISO/IEC 20000 standards and a member of several different international standard writing groups) have made absolutely invaluable contributions to this second edition and we are most appreciative of their input.

Further thanks go to Vicki Utting for getting this project going. Special thanks go to John Custy, Managing Consultant at JPC Group, Chris Evans, ICT Compliance Manager, London Fire Brigade, H.L. (Maarten) Souw RE, IT-Auditor, UWV and Agustin Lopez Neira, Lead Auditor and Trainer, ISO27000, for their early help and feedback. They gave the most careful reading of the book, and advice based on years of experience. Thanks as well to Susan Dobson for copy editing the book.

And finally, without both the technical and emotional support of Angela Wilde, the book would not have been started or finished.

CONTENTS

Contents

Contents

INTRODUCTION

This management guide provides an overview of the requirements of the implementation of a service management system that conforms to the requirements of ISO/IEC 20000-12011.

Implementing Service Quality based on ISO/IEC 20000 is aimed at CIOs, project managers, ISO/IEC 20000 consultants, auditors and implementers in IT consulting, IT service, and other companies which offer IT services and want to implement the Standard to show to their clients that they offer the highest standard of quality in their services.

This book is intended as a management guide on ISO/IEC 20000, so it has little information about the background and history of the ISO/IEC 20000 Standard. It is an overview of implementation, rather than a detailed implementation guide, and it is not a substitute for reading and studying the Standard itself.

CHAPTER 1: INTRODUCTION TO ISO/IEC 20000

The ISO/IEC 20000 Service Management Standard, first published by the organisations, ISO (International Organization for Standardization) and IEC (International Electrotechnical Commission) on 14 December 2005 and revised on 15 April 2011, is the internationally recognised standard in IT service management. The ISO/IEC 20000 series is based on the BS 15000 series developed by the British Standards Institution (BSI).

The goal of ISO/IEC 20000 is to establish a common reference standard for all companies which provide IT services for internal or external customers. Another goal is to promote a common terminology. Thus, the Standard has a significant contribution in the communication between service providers, suppliers and customers.

What are the benefits of implementing and certifying according to ISO/IEC 20000?

These will, of course, differ from organisation to organisation. However, the following list is a pretty good representation of the common results:

- Improved quality of service
- Increased business, and customer, confidence
- Improved reputation, consistency and interoperability
- Continuous improvement assured
- Optimised and controlled costs, through transparent and optimised structures
- Management and staff understand their roles and processes better

- Market advantage through a certificate issued by a recognised, independent, certification body
- Service management integrated into the overall business processes.

The integrated process approach from the Service Management Framework ITIL® is carried over to the Standard. This framework is positioned in a process model, which becomes part of the quality management system and is an important tool in communication with customers. The framework illustrates what processes control and continuously improves the service delivery.

Even though there is a link between ISO/IEC 20000 and ITIL, they are not aligned. The key differences are as follows:

- ISO/IEC 20000 requirements are completely independent of organisational structure or size, while ITIL includes advice and options for some aspects of organisational structure.
- In ISO/IEC 20000, service reporting is a separate process, while ITIL makes reference to service reports as part of the continual service improvement stage as well as part of every process.
- Service continuity and availability management have been combined in ISO/IEC 20000, while in ITIL, service continuity and availability management are separate processes.
- In ISO/IEC 20000, capacity management is presented as a single unit, while in ITIL three aspects are described: business, service and component capacity management.
- Financial management within ISO/IEC 20000 focuses purely on budgeting and accounting activities, while ITIL includes in-depth discussion on pricing and

charging, which, of course, cannot be mandatory activities in any organisation.

· ITIL includes functional areas and 26 processes in life cycle stages while ISO/IEC 20000 focuses on the service management system (SMS) and 13 processes (no functions).

Figure 1: Relationship between ISO/IEC 20000 and ITIL

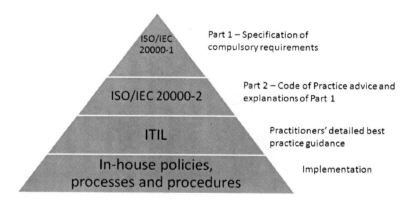

CHAPTER 2: SERVICE QUALITY AND ISO/IEC 20000

What is quality?

According to the American Society for Quality (ASQ), it is defined as follows: 'A subjective term for which each person or sector has its own definition. In technical usage, quality can have two meanings:

1. The characteristics of a product or service that bear on its ability to satisfy stated or implied needs.

2. A product or service free of deficiencies.'

The Standard ISO9000 defines quality in the following way: 'Degree to which a set of inherent characteristics fulfils requirements'. (Note: The term 'quality' can be used with adjectives, such as poor, good or excellent. 'Inherent', as opposed to 'assigned', means existing in something, especially as a permanent characteristic.)

The common element of all quality definitions is that the quality of a product or service refers to the perception of the degree to which the product or service meets the customer's expectations.

Service quality is the first concept that must be considered for any organisation seeking to implement a service management system (SMS).

Quality in IT service management is one of the most important parts of the delivery of IT services. Consequently, service quality management plays an increasingly important role in the global IT service management environment.

Quality is achieved when the client is experiencing an added value from its IT business. The warranty of this added value in terms of availability, performance, continuity, and security in the daily operations, is as important as the technical support of applications and automated tasks.

CHAPTER 3: THE ISO/IEC 20000 FAMILY AND EMERGING RELATED STANDARDS

The Standard is organised in the following five parts:

1. Part 1: ISO/IEC 20000-1:2011 – Service Management System Requirements
2. Part 2: ISO/IEC 20000-2:2012 – Guidance on the Application of Service Management Systems
3. Part 3: ISO/IEC20000-3:2012 – Guidance on Scope Definition and Applicability of ISO/IEC 20000-1
4. Part 4: ISO/IEC TR 20000-4:2010 – Process Reference Model
5. Part 5: ISO/IEC TR 20000-5:2010 – Exemplar Implementation Plan for ISO/IEC 20000-1.

All five parts can be found on the IT Governance website, *www.itgovernance.co.uk/catalog/47*.

In the meantime, several other parts are currently under development within the ISO/IEC 20000 series, as well as other standards relating to the ISO/IEC 20000 series:

- ISO/IEC 20000-7 – Application of ISO/IEC 20000-1 to the Cloud
- ISO/IEC 20000-10 – Concepts and terminology of ISO/IEC 20000-1
- ISO/IEC 20000-11 – Guidance on the relationship between ISO/IEC 20000-1 and related frameworks
- ISO/IEC 90006 – Guidelines for the application of ISO9001:2008 to IT service management
- ISO/IEC 27013 – Guidelines on the integrated implementation of ISO/IEC 20000-1 and ISO/IEC 27001

3: The ISO/IEC 20000 Family and Emerging Related Standards

- ISO/IEC CD 19770-3 – Software asset management – Part 3: Software entitlement tag
- ISO/IEC CD 19770-5 – Software asset management – Part 5: Overview and vocabulary

Other standards relating to the ISO/IEC 20000 series have already been published:

- ISO/IEC 15504-8 – An exemplar assessment model for IT service management
- ISO/IEC 19770-1:2012 – Software asset management – Part 1: Processes and tiered assessment of conformance
- ISO/IEC 19770-2:2009 – Software asset management – Part 2: Software identification tag.

Figure 2: ISO/IEC 20000 series and related frameworks

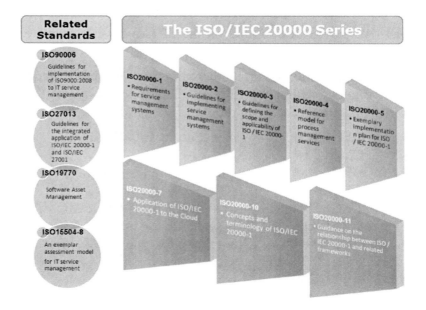

3: The ISO/IEC 20000 Family and Emerging Related Standards

ISO/IEC 20000-1:2011

ISO/IEC 20000-1:2011 is the second edition of ISO/IEC 20000-1. It replaces the 2005 edition. The main differences are:

- Nine additional pages, including an expanded introduction, additional requirements, and new and updated definitions.
- A new title: 'Service Management System – Requirements' instead of Specification.
- Closer alignment to ISO 9001 Quality Management Systems – Requirements.
- Closer alignment to ISO/IEC 27001 Information Security Management – Requirements.
- Closer alignment to the ITIL best practice framework.
- Addition of many more definitions, updates to some definitions and removal of two definitions.
- Introduction of the term 'Service Management System' (SMS).
- Combining clauses 3 and 4 of the ISO/IEC 20000-1:2005 edition, to put all management system requirements into one clause.
- Clarification of the requirements for the governance of processes operated by other parties.
- Clarification of the requirements for defining the scope of the SMS.
- Clarification of the application of the Standard.
- Clarification that the PDCA methodology applies to the SMS, including the service management processes and the services.
- Introduction of new requirements for the design and transition of new, or changed, services.

- Nine clauses, instead of 10 – the release management clause has been removed and integrated into the control processes clause.
- Service request has been added to the resolution processes clause in the incident management process.
- More specific documentation management requirements.
- More explicit budgeting and accounting section, including the service components that should be included.
- More precise details on the content of contracts with suppliers.

Figure 3: Comparison of ISO/IEC 20000-1:2005 and 2011

ISO/IEC 20000-1:2005	ISO/IEC 20000-1:2011
Scope	Scope
Terms and definitions	Normative references
Requirements for a management system	Terms and definitions
Planning and implementing service management	Service management system general requirements
Planning and implementing new or changed services	Design and transition of new or changed services

ISO/IEC 20000-1:2005	ISO/IEC 20000-1:2011
Service delivery processes – SLM, service reporting, service continuity and availability, budgeting and accounting for IT services, capacity management, information security management	Service delivery processes – SLM, service reporting, service continuity and availability, budgeting and accounting for IT services, capacity management, information security management
Relationship processes – business relationship management, supplier management	Relationship processes – business relationship management, supplier management
Resolution processes – incident and problem	Resolution processes – incident and service request, problem
Control processes – configuration and change	Control processes – configuration and change, release and deployment
Release process – release management	

ISO/IEC 20000-2:2012

ISO/IEC 20000-2:2012 is a revision of ISO/IEC 20000-2:2005, with a new title, 'Guidance on application'. It was released 15 February 2012. The structure of the document is identical to ISO/IEC 20000-1:2011. For every process, the following information is included in the Standard:

- Intent of the requirements
- Concepts

- Explanation of requirements
- Documents and records
- Authorities and responsibilities
- Interfaces and integration.

ISO/IEC 20000-3:2012

ISO/IEC 20000-3:2012 includes practical guidance on scope definition, applicability and demonstration of conformity to the requirements in ISO/IEC 20000-1.

It can also assist organisations that need specific advice as to whether ISO/IEC 20000-1 is applicable to their circumstances.

The guidance in the Standard takes the form of practical examples, typical scenarios and recommendations that show how the scope of an SMS can be defined, whether or not you have experience.

With service management processes crossing many organisational, legal and national boundaries, as well as different time zones, these and other issues can make the application of scope a complex stage in the service provider's use of ISO/IEC 20000-1. ISO/IEC 20000-3 will assist in this.

ISO/IEC 20000-3:2012 also assists in planning service improvements and in preparation for a conformity assessment against ISO/IEC 20000-1. It supplements the guidance on the application of ISO/IEC 20000-1 given in ISO/IEC 20000-2.

ISO/IEC TR 20000-4:2010

The purpose of ISO/IEC TR 20000-4:2010 is to facilitate the development of a process assessment model, according to ISO/IEC 15504 process assessment principles. ISO/IEC 15504-1 describes the concepts and terminology used for process assessment. ISO/IEC 15504-2 describes the requirements for the conduct of an assessment, and a measurement scale for assessing process capability.

The process reference model provided in ISO/IEC TR 20000-4:2010 is a logical representation of the elements of the processes within service management, that can be performed at a basic level. Using the reference model in a practical application might require additional elements suited to the environment and circumstances.

ISO/IEC TR 20000-5:2010

ISO/IEC TR 20000-5:2010 is an exemplar implementation plan. It provides guidance on how to implement a service management system to fulfil the requirements of ISO/IEC 20000-1, and is for service providers who are planning service improvements and are intending to use ISO/IEC 20000 as a business goal. It could also be useful for those advising service providers on how to best achieve the requirements of ISO/IEC 20000-1.

ISO/IEC TR 20000-5:2010 includes advice for service providers on a suitable order in which to plan and implement improvements. It is suggested that a generic three-phase approach is used to implement a service management system. The phased approach provides a structured framework to prioritise and manage the implementation activities.

ISO/IEC TR 20000-5:2010 is for guidance only. The service provider has the option of choosing their own implementation sequence to implement a service management system.

ISO/IEC 20000-7

ISO/IEC 20000-7. Information technology – Service management – Part 7: Guidance on the application of ISO/IEC 20000-1 to the Cloud. Currently under development, this standard will provide guidance on the application of Part 1 to the Cloud. It will explain the importance of an SMS for Cloud service providers and demonstrate the benefits of ISO/IEC 20000 for both Cloud service providers and Cloud service consumers. It is anticipated that Cloud service models, such as SAAS, PAAS and IAAS, would be included, as well as deployment models, such as private, community, public and hybrid-Cloud configurations.

ISO/IEC 20000-10

Currently under development, this part will focus on the terminology and concepts of IT service management related to 20000.

ISO/IEC 20000-11

Currently under development, this part will provide guidance on how ITIL is related to ISO/IEC 20000-1. ISO/IEC 20000 and ITIL are not based on each other, which is a common misconception. There is some alignment between the two but ISO/IEC 20000 and ITIL serve different purposes and are, therefore, different in intent, format, structure, style and details.

ISO/IEC 15504-8:2010

This Process Assessment Model (PAM) is for performing a conformance assessment in accordance with the requirements of ISO/IEC 15504-2. It enables implemented processes of ISO/IEC 20000-1 to be assessed according to the requirements of ISO/IEC 15504-2.

ISO/IEC 90006

This technical report, planned for 2013, will bring guidance on the application of ISO9001:2000 to the latest version of ISO/IEC 20000-1. It intends to establish a common and worldwide interpretation of the commonalities and differences between the requirements of both ISO9001 and ISO/IEC 20000-1. It intends to support enterprise adoption and the audit of management systems developed, following the requirements of one, or both, standards.

ISO/IEC 27013

This standard is still under development. Once published, it will provide guidance on implementing an integrated information security and IT service management system, based on the ISO/IEC 27001 and ISO/IEC 20000-1 Standards respectively, since these management systems are felt to complement and support each other.

ISO/IEC 19770

ISO19770 is an international set of standards for Software Asset Management (SAM). SAM is a requirement for organisations that want to effectively manage processes and procedures, to ensure compliance with legal requirements and software contracts. ISO/IEC 19770 has a strong affiliation with ISO/IEC 20000. It is constructed in six main sections:

1. Control environment
2. Planning and implementation
3. Inventory
4. Verification and compliance
5. Operations management
6. Life cycle.

CHAPTER 4: FRAMEWORKS AND MANAGEMENT SYSTEM INTEGRATION

ISO/IEC 20000 is designed to harmonise with management systems based on the Deming Cycle, like ISO9001, ISO14001 and ISO27001. This makes it possible to develop a completely integrated management system that can achieve certification to ISO/IEC 20000, ISO9001, ISO14001 and ISO27001.

ISO9000

ISO9000 refers to a set of standards of quality and continuous quality management, established by the International Organization for Standardization (ISO). They can be applied to any organisation or activity producing goods or services.

The rules include both the minimum contents and the specific guidelines and implementation tools, such as audit methods. ISO9000 specifies how an organisation operates, its standards of quality, delivery times and service levels. There are more than 20 elements in the ISO9000 Standards that relate to the way the systems should operate.

ISO14000

Today, more than ever, environmental management is a crucial issue for the success of any business. For many, the answer is an Environmental Management System (EMS), a framework for managing the impacts that occur in the environment. In addition to reducing negative impacts on the environment, an EMS can reduce costs, improve efficiency and provide competitive advantage to companies.

ISO14000 is an internationally accepted standard that helps to establish an effective EMS. It is designed to strike a balance between maintaining profitability and reducing environmental impacts. ISO14000 focuses on any organisation of any size or sector that is looking to improve its environmental impact and to comply with legislation on the environment.

ISO/IEC 27000

Information is a vital asset to success and continuity in the market for any organisation. The security of that information, and those systems that process it, are therefore a prime target for all organisations.

For the proper management of information security, there must exist an information security management system that addresses this task in a methodical, documented way and is based on clear objectives of security and risk assessment.

ISO/IEC 27000 is a set of standards developed by ISO (International Organization for Standardization) and IEC (International Electrotechnical Commission), which provide a framework for the management of information security that can be used by any organisation, public or private, large or small.

As of the publication date, the current standards include:

- *ISO/IEC 27000* – Information security management systems – Overview and vocabulary
- *ISO/IEC 27001* – Information security management systems – Requirements

- *ISO/IEC 27002* – Code of practice for information security management
- *ISO/IEC 27003* – Information security management system implementation guidance
- *ISO/IEC 27004* – Information security management – Measurement
- *ISO/IEC 27005* – Information security risk management
- *ISO/IEC 27006* – Requirements for bodies providing audit and certification of information security management systems
- *ISO/IEC 27007* – Guidelines for information security management systems auditing (focused on the management system)
- *ISO/IEC 27008* – Guidance for auditors on ISMS controls (focused on the information security controls)
- *ISO/IEC 27010* – Information security management for inter-sector and inter-organisational communications
- *ISO/IEC 27011* – Information security management guidelines for telecommunications organisations based on ISO/IEC 27002
- *ISO/IEC 27031* – Guidelines for information and communications technology readiness for business continuity
- *ISO/IEC 27032* – Guideline for cybersecurity
- *ISO/IEC 27033-1* – Network security – Part 1: Overview and concepts
- *ISO/IEC 27033-2* – Network security – Part 2: Guidelines for the design and implementation of network security

- *ISO/IEC 27033-3* – Network security – Part 3: Reference networking scenarios – Threats, design techniques and control issues
- *ISO/IEC 27034-1* – Application security – Part 1: Overview and concepts
- *ISO/IEC 27035* – Information security incident management
- *ISO 27799* – Information security management in health using ISO/IEC 27002

There are additional standards under development:

- *ISO/IEC 27013* – Guideline on the integrated implementation of ISO/IEC 20000-1 and ISO/IEC 27001
- *ISO/IEC 27014* – Governance of information security
- *ISO/IEC 27015* – Information security management guidelines for financial services
- *ISO/IEC 27016* – Organisational economics
- *ISO/IEC 27017* – Guidelines on information security controls for the use of Cloud Computing services based on ISO/IEC 27002
- *ISO/IEC 27018* – Code of practice for data protection controls for public Cloud Computing services
- *ISO/IEC 27019* – Information security management guidelines based on ISO/IEC 27002 for process control systems specific to the energy industry
- *ISO/IEC 27034-2* – Application security – Part 2: Organisation normative framework
- *ISO/IEC 27034-3* – Application security – Part 3: Application security management process

- *ISO/IEC 27034-4* – Application security – Part 4: Application security validation
- *ISO/IEC 27034-5* – Application security – Part 5: Protocols and application security controls data structure
- *ISO/IEC 27034-6* – Application security– Part 6: Security guidance for specific applications
- *ISO/IEC 27036-1* – Information security for supplier relationships – Part 1: Overview and concepts
- *ISO/IEC 27036-2* – Information security for supplier relationships – Part 2: Common requirements
- *ISO/IEC 27036-3* – Information security for supplier relationships – Part 3: Guidelines for ICT supply chain security
- *ISO/IEC 27037* – Guidelines for identification, collection and/or acquisition and preservation of digital evidence.
- *ISO/IEC 27038* – Security techniques – Specification for Digital Redaction
- *ISO/IEC 27039* – Security techniques – Selection, deployment and operations of intrusion detection systems
- *ISO/IEC 27040* – Security techniques – Storage security
- *ISO/IEC 27044* – Security Information and Event Management (SIEM)

ITIL

ITIL can be defined as a set of best practices in a series of publications that describe a possible implementation of IT service management (ITSM). ITIL outlines an extensive set of management procedures, designed to help organisations achieve quality and efficiency of IT operations. These procedures are supplier independent and have been developed to serve as a guide that includes all infrastructure, development and IT operations. ITIL is owned and maintained by the Cabinet Office.

COBIT®

COBIT (Control Objectives for Information and Related Technology) was first released in 1996. The current version, *COBIT 5*, was published in 2012. COBIT 5 helps enterprises to create optimal value from IT by maintaining a balance between realising benefits and optimising risk levels and resource use.

COBIT 5 enables information and related technology to be governed and managed in a holistic manner for the whole enterprise, taking in the full end-to-end business and functional areas of responsibility, considering the IT-related interests of internal and external stakeholders.

It is based on processes and focuses heavily on control and less on execution, i.e. shows what you get without focus on the how. The new version has a clarifying character, integrating COBIT 4, Val IT and Risk IT in a process reference model. Also, COBIT 5 has been adapted to align with the ISO/IEC 38500 IT Governance and the GEIT framework under the ITGI (IT Governance Institute).

COBIT 5 brings together the five principles that allow the enterprise to build an effective governance and management framework based on a holistic set of seven enablers that optimises information and technology investment and use for the benefit of stakeholders.

Six Sigma®

Developed by Motorola in 1986, but truly gained recognition in 1995 when GE's Jack Welch utilised the principles to underpin the overall business strategy. Six Sigma focuses on improving the quality of process outputs. Central to the Six Sigma activities is the identification and removal of defects (errors) and minimising variance in production and business processes.

Through the use of quality management principles and statistical methodologies, the outcome of a Six Sigma process is cost reduction or profit increase. Utilising the concept of a normal curve and standard deviation, which uses the Greek sigma (σ) character, six standard deviations incorporate 99.99966% of the area. Thus, if an organisation has achieved 'a Six Sigma process', it is expected that the product is statistically free of defects (3.4 defects per million).

The management methodology follows one of two systems: DMAIC for existing processes or DMADV for new product/process designs.

The DMAIC method has five phases

- *Define* the problem and project goals
- *Measure* critical aspects of the current process and collect required data

- *Analyse* the data for cause-and-effect relationships and define the root cause of the defect
- *Improve* the current process to mitigate the defect
- *Control* the future state (e.g. proactively monitor to prevent future defects).

DMADV is also known as DFSS (Design for Six Sigma) and it, too, has five phases.

- *Define* goals consistent with customer requirements
- *Measure* and identify critical aspects for quality products, risk reduction, production capabilities
- *Analyse* to develop alternatives as well as criteria to select the final design
- *Design* the process and optimise; design the validation process
- *Verify* the design via pilots, implement and transition to the process owners.

CMMI® for Services

An offshoot of the Capability Maturity Model Integration from Carnegie Mellon and the Software Engineering Institute, CMMI for Services (CMMI-SVC) is another quality framework with a goal of improving processes in order to provide outstanding services.

CMMI-SVC is based on the concepts from CMMI, as well as ITIL, ISO/IEC 20000, COBIT and the Information Technology Services Capability Maturity Model (ITSCMM). As such, this model describes the activities and best practices to establish, deliver and manage services.

Applicable to IT, as well as healthcare, public sector services, the transportation industry and other service industries, this model defines the practices to address the scope of service activities including work management, process management, service establishment, service delivery and support and the supporting processes.

Many organisations have already incorporated an aspect of the original maturity model in their assessment activities utilising the five maturity levels (Levels 1 to 5) of Initial, Repeatable, Defined, Managed and Optimized. Capability levels are a bit different. There are four capability levels (Levels 0 to 3):

- **Level 0: Incomplete** – a process that is not performed or only partially performed
- **Level 1: Performed** – a process that achieves the necessary and expected work product or outcome
- **Level 2: Managed** – a process that is planned and executed according to policy, has adequate resources, produces expected outcomes, has stakeholders; additionally it is monitored, controlled and reviewed
- **Level 3: Defined** – a managed process has a defined set of procedures and policies, follows a defined standard and is consistently followed; a defined process has much greater detail (granularity) in the description, inputs, outputs, activities, roles, measures, etc. ...

CHAPTER 5: REQUIREMENTS FOR A SERVICE MANAGEMENT SYSTEM

In order to successfully realise service quality, the first process group of the ISO/IEC 20000 Standard defines the principles of a successful implementation of the service management system. This service management system allows us to manage and implement our IT services effectively.

The Standard is asking for a service management system which satisfies the following:

- Management responsibility
- Governance of processes operated by other parties
- Documentation management (policies and plans, service documentation, procedures, process and process control records)
- Resource management.

How can we build such a service management system that covers the above requirements? In which documents/process descriptions do we have to file the requirements for compliance?

Management responsibility

The goal is to establish the responsibilities for implementing the service management system at the top level of the service provider. Management must be aware of its responsibility and support the service management system and its structures, which are necessary for the establishment and maintenance of services. By showing clear leadership, commitment and active actions, the top management must provide a verifiable proof that it can meet its obligations to develop, implement and optimise service management capabilities.

The responsibilities of the management are listed below:

- Establish the service management policies, objectives and implementation plans (policies and procedures).
- Convey the importance of the achievement of the service management objectives.
- Make sure that the customer requirements are determined and measures are taken to meet those needs.
- Appoint a member of management who is responsible for co-ordinating and managing all services.
- Identify and deploy resources for the planning, implementation, monitoring, review and improvement of service delivery and service management.
- Setting up and implementation of a risk management for service management organisations and services.

Practical recommendations on the implementation of management responsibility

To fulfil the above commitments, the responsibility for the service management system has to be assigned to a member of management with sufficient authority. This person will be supported by a management group that contributes to decision making. The defined management individual is thus also the owner of the entire service management system.

5: Requirements for a Service Management System

Service management policy

In the service management policy, we establish the principles of management structure, which should be adopted as a mandatory policy for further application in all other policies and processes.

The service management policy documents the intention of the management, to align the offered services – documented in the service catalogue – to generate customer value and to achieve business goals.

The consistent focus on the established frameworks and standards defines how the strategy of the company is achieved.

Service management plan

The IT service management plan is a document used to structure the yearly planning of service management. It defines tasks, deadlines and responsibilities for the successful completion of various activities within the IT organisation. The responsible management individual determines the framework for this planning, in close co-ordination with the various process owners. This annual plan is the basis for the establishment of the continuous improvement process – Plan, Do, Check, Act (PDCA) – according to ISO/IEC 20000.

The implementation of the plan can only be successful if it is agreed with stakeholders, business, key suppliers and managers within the organisation.

The services offered by the service management organisation must be documented in a service catalogue and written in business language.

This catalogue provides the framework for all activities. To properly exercise each task, appropriate policies are involved.

A service management plan should be prepared, in which the different individual goals for the coming fiscal year are recorded. These include the surveys, budget planning, continuity tests, dates and responsibilities of the various management activities, such as change advisory boards, process reviews and customer satisfaction. It also sets deadlines and responsibilities for the successful completion of various activities.

Governance of processes operated by other parties

Many organisations may choose other parties to manage aspects of their processes, such as another internal group, customer or supplier. The service provider needs to demonstrate overall governance of those processes managed by the other party.

Specifically, the service provider must be accountable for the process and have the necessary authority to demand compliance to the process. Process definition and dependencies (interfaces) will be controlled by the service provider, as well as the overall performance. Improvements will be controlled by the service provider.

This section sounds very similar to the supplier management process requirements and, in fact, when the other party is a supplier, the supplier management process requirements are germane. But, when the other party is an internal group, service level management requirements will manage the customer or other internal party. This section clearly requires the service provider to demonstrate overall governance in order to fulfil all aspects of the SMS.

Documentation management

The service provider must provide the documentation and records which support the management processes. This allows effective planning, operation and control of the service management processes.

Documentation management provides a complete system for seamless control of all documents and information. Documents and data are assigned to the systems used, for the proper handling of the service management. This system is controlled, managed and updated via the company's intranet. We need a clearly defined responsible person for all documents, data and systems.

All relevant activities have to be captured in the form of records, which have to be easy to find. Records are plans, protocols, reports and logs of business activities. They are of great help for the continuous improvement (PDCA) process of an IT organisation.

The service manager must ensure that the service management system can be audited. All those documents and records which are provided as part of a document management system, are necessary for this process.

The following specifications are to be met in terms of documentation:

- Policies and implementation plans have to be documented
- Service Level Agreements (SLAs) must be documented
- Processes and procedures, in accordance with this standard, shall be documented
- Records of the effective operation of the processes must be documented

- A document management system that covers the procedures and responsibilities for the preparation, review, release, maintenance, disposal and management of documents and records must be created.

Practical recommendations on the implementation of documentation management

For the creation and management of documents and records, a process needs to be set up. The documents are the basis and foundation for evidence that the service management directives are complied with.

Two essential elements need to be distinguished between:

- Documents that hold the plans and intentions
- Records that demonstrate the effective implementation.

It has to be demonstrated that service management does not exist only on paper, but is actually followed in all processes. This proof must be provided holistically. It is the responsibility of the management that all the policies and processes are documented, communicated, followed, monitored and improved.

Documentation policy

To achieve the service management objectives needs firm guidelines and process documentation. An essential foundation is achieved through the creation of a documentation management policy, which provides the guidelines and principles for the effective implementation of the ISO/IEC 20000 Standard.

Documentation structure

To get a complete overview of the service offering, a service catalogue, with all active IT services, should be created and maintained. The service catalogue serves as a key document to set the customer expectations. Because of the importance of this document, the customer and the support staff of the service provider should have access to the service catalogue.

Figure 4: Table of necessary policies, plans and processes

ISO/IEC 20000-1:2011	Policies	Plans	Process
Scope			
Normative references			
Terms and definitions			
Service management system general requirements	Service management, continual improvement	Service management, internal audit	
Design and transition of new or changed services		New service	

5: Requirements for a Service Management System

ISO/IEC 20000-1:2011	Policies	Plans	Process
Service delivery processes – SLM, service reporting, service continuity and availability, budgeting and accounting for IT services, capacity management, information security management	Service level, service reporting, service continuity and availability, budgeting and accounting for IT services, capacity management (all included in service management), information security management	Service reporting, service continuity, service availability, budgeting, accounting, capacity, security	Service level, service reporting, service continuity and availability, budgeting and accounting for IT services, capacity management, information security management
Relationship processes – business relationship management, supplier management	Business relationship, supplier (all included in service management)		Business relationship, supplier
Resolution processes – incident and service request, problem	Incident and service request, problem (all included in service management)		Incident and service request, problem

ISO/IEC 20000-1:2011	Policies	Plans	Process
Control processes – configuration and change, release and deployment	Configuration and change, release and deployment (all included in service management)	Configuration, change, release and deployment	Configuration and change, release and deployment

Resource management

An appropriate management system should ensure that all those people who have a management role within the service, have the right skills for their role. To do this, the skills and abilities required to perform each role included in your service management system should be defined.

The Standard asks for the following specifications:

• All service management roles and responsibilities must be defined, with the necessary skills for effective implementation.
• The competence of staff and training needs should be reviewed periodically.
• Top management are responsible for ensuring that all employees are aware of the relevance and importance of their activities, and their contribution to the service management targets.

Practical recommendations on the implementation of resource management

The dynamic and technological advancements in the area of service management require ongoing education and training of employees. As part of the annual target agreements, and the requirements of the service-management planning, the training needs of the staff should be defined and a yearly training plan developed. All training sessions should be reviewed for their effectiveness.

To determine specific needs, the service provider shall determine in advance the specific competencies for each role in service management. There should be detailed records for each employee on their training, skills and experience.

Close co-operation with the human resources department is recommended, as they generally already have details of the training levels of all personnel.

Professional staff development

The service provider must continuously develop the professional skills of its workforce. The following areas should be specifically addressed:

- Recruitment
- Planning
- Training and staff development.

All relevant aspects of service management, team collaboration and leadership skills need special attention, in terms of training and staff development.

It is recommended that teams are formed with active employees and new employees, to provide the agreed services with those combined capabilities. Similarly, a balance between internal (know-how) and external employees (specific expertise) has to be found.

CHAPTER 6: SCOPE DEFINITION

When seeking certification, a service provider has to decide on the scope of the service to be audited, and agree this with the ISO/IEC 20000 auditor, in advance of the audit. For certification audits, an RCB (Registered Certification Body) is responsible for validating the scope, as a prerequisite to the certification process.

The scoping requirement for a service management system (SMS) is contained in clause 4.5.1 of the ISO/IEC 20000-1:2011 specification. Detailed information and guidance on creating the scope statement can be found in ISO/IEC 20000-3 (Guidance on Scope Definition and Applicability of ISO/IEC 20000-1).

An organisation can seek certification for the entire organisation, or part of that organisation. For the certification, it is unimportant whether the processes within the scope of the audit are performed entirely by a single organisation, or performed partly by other organisations.

The scoping statement should explicitly cover:

- The services encompassed by the audit
- Any geographical or location boundaries (e.g. a site, a regional or national boundary)
- Organisational or functional boundaries
- Any outsourced process components (e.g. the performance data collection elements of capacity management).

As a guideline, a service provider should be able to easily provide the following:

- A clear definition of the scope of the services and infrastructure within the scope of ISO/IEC 20000 audit.
- The interfaces between processes, with clarity on how they are controlled by the service provider.
- Information on the role of, and the interfaces to other organisations, involved in the overall service delivery, including any of the service provider's customers and suppliers.

A typical template for the scope definition is as follows:

The <service(s)> to <customers> within the <technical> and <organisational> boundaries of <legal entity> at <locations>.

Examples for scopes of already certified organisations can be found at
http://www.isoiec20000certification.com/home/ISOCertifie dOrganizations/ISOCountryListings.aspx

ISO/IEC TR 20000-3:2012

ISO/IEC 20000-3:2012 provides guidance on scope definition and the applicability of ISO/IEC 20000-1.

It additionally covers demonstration of conformity to the requirements in ISO/IEC 20000-1. Guidance on the different types of conformity assessment and assessment standards is included.

The Standard will help you establish if ISO/IEC 20000-1 is applicable to your organisation's circumstances. The guidance in the Standard takes the form of practical examples, typical scenarios and recommendations that shows how the scope of an SMS can be defined, whether or not you have experience.

With service management processes crossing many organisational, legal and national boundaries, as well as different times zones, these and other issues can make the application of scope a complex stage in the service provider's use of ISO/IEC 20000-1. ISO/IEC 20000-3 will assist with this endeavour.

ISO/IEC 20000-3:2012 also assists in planning service improvements and in preparation for a conformity assessment against ISO/IEC 20000-1. It supplements the guidance on the application of ISO/IEC 20000-1 given in ISO/IEC 20000-2.

CHAPTER 7: GAP ANALYSIS

As with all large projects that are carried out in a company, we have to first show the objectives of the project (the 'What'). On the other hand, the advantages and benefits for the enterprise (the 'Why') need to be presented to the top management, before starting the ISO/IEC 20000 project.

ISO/IEC 20000 should not be seen as an end in itself. Left like this, the IT staff would be only stressed out, without creating any value for them. The ISO/IEC 20000 certification has to be seen rather as the result of a larger IT service management programme. This overall programme targets the customer focus and efficiency of the IT organisation and transforms it into an IT service organisation.

An ISO/IEC 20000 project is not a small task and should be planned as a project which co-ordinates and manages multiple projects from the beginning. Before beginning such planning, a gap analysis should be executed, to determine the starting position. The following factors should be considered essential in such an analysis:

- The project management system
- The process management system
- The document management system
- The service catalogue
- The service management tools
- The education level of the service management teams involved.

The study of the process maturity of the IT service organisation is important initial information for the

ISO/IEC 20000 programme. This measurement can provide information on the expected efforts and tasks in the ISO/IEC 20000 implementation. Furthermore, these measurements should be repeated at least annually, to monitor the continuous improvement of IT service management processes. The results of those measurements should be an integral part of the process improvement plan.

The main issues for the gap analysis come naturally from the Standard itself, namely from Part 1 and 2 of ISO/IEC 20000. Apart from these two sources, that should be used on the start of the analysis, there are other tools that should be considered.

CHAPTER 8: PLANNING AND IMPLEMENTING SERVICE MANAGEMENT

During planning and implementation of the service management requirements, processes and defined responsibilities have to be taken into account. A service management system (SMS) is the basis for this. The development of a SMS is a demanding task and requires an understanding of the purpose, policies and objectives, and the processes involved. This relationship is understood as planning and implementation of service management. For a successful implementation of the service management system, the Standard makes reference to the established Deming Cycle: Plan, Do, Check, Act.

The Deming Cycle is not only to apply as the overall service management system, but is regarded as the basis for the implementation of all subsequent service management processes.

Plan

The goal of this process is to plan the implementation and operation of the service management system. The overall service management plan must cover at least the following topics:

- The scope of service management within the service provider.
- The IT service management objectives to be achieved.
- The necessary processes, such as implementation, deployment, changes and improvements to the service management process.

- Management roles and responsibilities for senior management, process owner and supplier management.
- Interfaces between the service management processes and the way the activities are co-ordinated.
- Implementation of service management processes in concrete activities.
- A method which identifies, evaluates and manages risks.
- Resources and necessary budget.
- Methods for management, auditing and improving service quality.

For the successful implementation of these plans, we need clear management statements and documented responsibilities for the review, approval, communication, implementation and maintenance of the necessary plans. All process-specific plans must be compliant with the overall service management plan.

Do

The goal of this process is to establish the service management objectives and the service management plan. The service management plan has to be implemented as follows:

- Allocation of budgets, roles and responsibilities
- Managing budgets and resources
- Co-ordination of service management processes
- Selection and training of employees, and effective measures against staff turnover
- Leading teams, including the service desk and the operational business
- Documentation and monitoring of plans, policies and procedures for the various processes

- Identification and treatment of service risks.

After implementing the service management plan, the focus needs to be on the operation and ongoing improvement of the service management processes. Practice has shown that the staff responsible for the implementation should be replaced by other appropriate staff for ongoing operations.

Check

In this process you have to monitor, measure and review the achievement of the objectives of service management and the service management plan.

The service provider must verify the effectiveness of the processes through monitoring and measuring:

- The management plan must be periodically reviewed
- These reviews should determine whether the service management requirements are compliant with the service management plan, and the requirements of ISO/IEC 20000
- An audit programme must be created.

The results of the review and testing are used as inputs for the next step in the Deming Cycle, 'Act'. Like this, you can achieve an improvement of service processes.

Act

The goal of this process is to increase the effectiveness and efficiency of service delivery and service management.

To identify actions for continuous improvement, the following conventions and definitions have to be taken into account:

- The management must establish and publish a policy that contains a clear definition of roles and responsibilities for the improvement of service activities.
- All aspects that do not conform to the service management plans should be eliminated.
- For the execution of all proposed service improvements, a Service Improvement Plan (SIP) must be created.
- For the processing of service improvements, a defined process is required.

Improvements to individual processes can be managed by each process owner. Major improvements, such as elimination of non-conformities with enterprise-wide scope, or improvements to more than one process, must be executed by one or more projects.

Before implementing a service improvement plan, baselines have to be created. Based on this data, a comparison can be made with the actual improvements.

Practical recommendations on the implementation of service management plans

The implementation of the Deming Cycle has to be established in the organisation. The documentation of all activities is absolutely essential for the successful application of the PDCA model. The output of each activity is also the input of the next activity. Communication between the processes is therefore of the utmost importance.

It is important that the service management employees have a deep knowledge of the service quality standards and the service management processes. This principle will ensure that measures can be taken at any time to improve the effectiveness and efficiency of service delivery.

Figure 5: The Deming Cycle

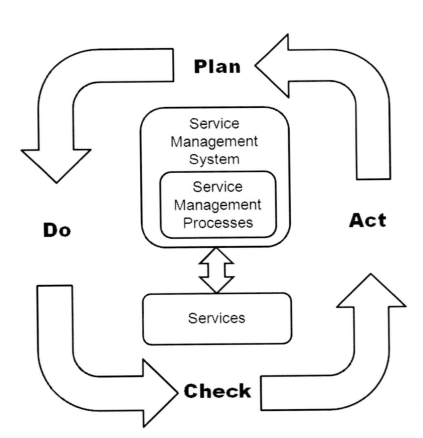

CHAPTER 9: DESIGN AND TRANSITION OF NEW OR CHANGED SERVICES

ISO/IEC 20000 has a separate process for planning and implementation of new, or changed, services. The objective here is the guarantee, to provide new and changed services for an agreed price and at the desired quality of service.

For new and modified services the following procedures apply:

- All new or changed services are implemented according to the PDCA cycle.
- The impact on costs and profitability has to be taken into account, for all new or changed services.
- The implementation of new or changed services, including the cancellation of a service, must be planned and formally approved by the change management.
- All CIs affected by the new or changed service are under the control of configuration management.

Specific requirements are provided in the major stages of deploying a new or changed service, which are:

- Plan new or changed services
- Design and development of new or changed services
- Transition of new or changed services.

It is easy to see the influence of the service life cycle as described by ITIL 2011, but ISO/IEC 20000-1 offers a very practical approach to managing the new or changed service. Note the application of the PDCA structure.

Plan new or changed services

Quite simply, all changes to services (or new services) require input from the customer or other interested parties. Interestingly, the service provider identifies the service requirements but t ey must be agreed with the customer. All requirements are assessed for their impact to financial, organisational, and technical areas, as well as the SMS. Any plans should reference:

- Responsibilities and risks
- Service provider and customer activities
- Communication and resources
- Timescales and service acceptance criteria
- Testing and dependencies
- Expected outcomes.

Planning should also be applied to the removal or transfer of services. Areas of consideration include the removal, archiving and transfer of data, as well as management of components and licenses. Security of those items will always underpin their management (see ISO/IEC 27001 for more detailed information).

Design and development of new or changed services

The design and development of a new or changed service requires consideration of authorities and responsibilities of the service provider and various other parties for the design, as well as consideration of the necessary resources. Within the resources, this phase will consider training and education, as well as the necessary capabilities to support the new or changed service.

Lastly, the effect of the new or changed service on the in-place services, policies, plans, SLAs, the SMS and service catalogue must be considered and addressed. Underpinning all design activities is the absolute assurance the new or changed service will meet the agreed requirements.

Transition of new or changed services

Once the design and development have been completed, the new or changed service must be tested to ensure the requirements have been met, as well as compatibility with the current infrastructure. These tests would be developed in the previous phase and carried out by independent resources. The test results are compared to previously defined service acceptance criteria. If a service is not meeting the criteria, a decision by the service provider and interested parties is made to either continue or not.

Release and deployment management, under the authority of change management, will deploy the new or changed service. As per the requirements of these two processes, the new or changed service would be assessed and evaluated as to the achieved outcomes versus the expected outcomes. Again, there is an opportunity to accept or reject the new or changed service if the performance is not acceptable.

CHAPTER 10: SERVICE DELIVERY PROCESSES

The service delivery core area includes the planning, and the tactical level, of IT service management. In this area, the actual service levels are defined and agreed, and reports on the services, provided.

Service delivery includes the following processes: service level management, service reporting, capacity, service continuity and availability, information security management, and budgeting for IT services and accounting.

Service level management

Service level management aims to define, agree, record and manage service levels. The service level management process must ensure that the entire scope of the services is agreed and documented:

- All IT services, with corresponding service level objectives and utilisation characteristics, must be defined.
- Any IT service must be documented in one or more Service Level Agreement (SLA).
- The SLAs must contain all supportive service agreements, supplier contracts, and procedures with all relevant parties.
- SLAs are placed under the control of the change management process.
- SLAs are maintained on the basis of regular reviews with the parties involved, in order to ensure that they remain relevant and effective.

- Service levels are monitored against the agreed objectives.
- Reasons for variations in the SLAs have to be investigated and reported.
- Identified improvement actions will be recorded and included in a service improvement plan.

Practical recommendations on the implementation of service level management

To meet the specifications of the service level management, a structured approach is recommended, in accordance with the following guidelines.

General requirements

The service level management process should not be executed in a formalistic and rigid way, but instead, should be flexible and proactive, and targeted for change. It is therefore of great importance to ensure a strong customer focus at all levels, and in all phases, of the service delivery. Customer satisfaction is a subjective measure and the achievement of agreed service objectives is understood as an objective measure – for that reason, appropriate attention should be given to the service perceived by customers or users.

This process controls the basic functions of the service provider and is the basis of providing services to the customer. The service provider should have sufficient information to really understand the business drivers and the requirements of the customer. The service level management process needs a fluent communication with the processes business relationship and supplier management.

Service catalogue

To get a complete overview of the service offering, a service catalogue, with all active IT services, should be created and maintained. The service catalogue serves as a key document to set the customer expectations. Because of the importance of this document, the customer and the support staff of the service provider should have access to the service catalogue.

Service level agreements

SLAs will be formally approved by the customers' representatives and the SLA manager of the service provider. The following elements should, at least, be maintained in an SLA:

- Brief service description in the language of the customer service objectives, communication and reporting.
- Contact addresses of the persons responsible for major incident and problem treatment, recovery or workaround.
- Service hours and specified exemptions, critical business times.
- Planned, and agreed upon, service interruptions, including notice period and number of interruptions per period.
- Responsibility of the customer, e.g. security.
- Service provider liability and obligation.
- Impact and priority policy, escalation and notification process.

- Sequence for complaints.
- Workload (upper and lower limits).
- Organisational processes (housekeeping procedures).
- Approach to a service interruption.
- Supporting and dependent services.
- Exceptions to the conditions defined in the SLA.
- Glossary.

Supportive service agreements

It is recommended that operational support services are necessary for the service provision to define as well. Those internal services should be agreed with the internal supplier with Operational Level Agreements (OLA), while the Underpinning Contracts (UC) are the agreements with the external provider. For this purpose, close co-operation with the supplier management process is required.

Service reporting

Service reporting has the goal to create reliable and accurate reports on time, to enable informed decisions and effective communications. All service reports must be clearly defined, with the intent and the purpose of the report, the target groups, and above all, its data sources. Identified needs from customer reporting requirements must be met.

Service reports contain the following data:

- Service performance against service level objectives
- List of violations and open issues
- Usage statistics and volume characteristics

- Performance records for important events, such as a major event
- Performance records of major changes
- Trend developments
- Satisfaction analysis
- Deviations from conformity.

Management decisions and corrective measures must be based on the results of the service supported reports and must be communicated to all relevant parties.

Practical recommendations on the implementation of service reporting

The success of all service management processes is dependent on the use of information from the service reports. The recommendations described in the following sections provide important clues.

Policy

Less is more. This applies especially for service reports. It is recommended that reports are prepared only on the basis of agreed and documented requirements from customers and internal IT management. Reports should also address the relationship with internal and external suppliers, for being able to review the entire service chain.

The service monitoring and reporting should also include current and historical measurements to detect the trends in service quality.

Purpose and quality review of service reports

To support the decision-making process effectively, all reports have to be timely, clear and precise. They also need to be matched with regard to presentation and detail, be easy to understand, and appropriate to the needs of the recipient.

The reports are subdivided into three different categories:

- Reactive reports on activities in the last period
- Proactive reports for advanced information, for example, warnings
- Planned activities, rolling change plan.

Service continuity and availability management

The two processes, service continuity and availability management, should ensure that the agreed objectives of availability and continuity to the customer, can be met.

To achieve this goal, the following specifications should be implemented:

- The availability and service continuity requirements must be based on business planning, SLAs and risk analysis.
- The requirements must take into account access rights, response times and end-to-end availability of the system components.
- The availability and service continuity plans should be reviewed at least annually, to ensure that the requirements can be met at all times.
- The availability and service continuity plans must be updated continually, to ensure that they meet the agreed business changes.

10: Service Delivery Processes

- The availability and service continuity plans need to be re-tested after every major change.

Practical recommendations on the implementation of service continuity and availability management

To meet the requirements of the service continuity and availability management, the following recommendations are made.

General recommendations

All activities and expenses, and the allocated resources for the implementation of the continuity and availability goals, are imperative, to co-ordinate with the requirements of the business.

Availability monitoring and activities

To monitor the services, you have to record the availability and the historical data for trend developments, in order to identify deviations from the defined objectives. It is also advisable to check initiated improvement measures to be followed, with regard to their effect.

The availability and the planned maintenance windows are to anticipate and to communicate to all stakeholders. Thus, targeted preventive maintenance can be carried out.

Service continuity strategy

The service provider must agree to create a strategy that complies with all the aims of service continuity. Part of this strategy is a risk assessment, based on the extent of damage and probability, that takes into account both service and special critical uptime.

It is recommended that the service provider establishes with each customer group, at least the following:

- Maximum acceptable amount of time without service
- Maximum acceptable amount of time with reduced service
- Accepted reduced service level during a defined recovery period.

The service continuity strategy must be continuously reviewed, at least annually, together with business representatives.

All changes to the strategy must be agreed formally and implemented as part of the change management.

Service continuity plan and test

The service provider shall ensure that the continuity plans take into account the dependencies of service and system components, and document them. The necessary back-up data, related documents, as well as software, equipment and staff, must be available quickly and reliably after a major service interruption, or a disaster. At least one copy of the service continuity documents must also be stored, together with the necessary equipment, in a safe, secluded place. This place could be a secondary data centre or a recovery site, the importance here is that it is not in the same place as the original service.

To ensure that the service continuity strategies can be reviewed, and the measures remain manageable by the service employees, the disaster recovery plans have to be tested regularly. These tests include the customer and external suppliers alike. Failed tests must be corrected and verified. All service continuity plans and related documents must be placed under the control of change management.

The service continuity plans also have to assign, clearly, the responsibility for initiating the continuity scenarios. Thus, it is recommended that the incident manager receives clear instructions when they have to call for crisis management, when a disturbance develops to a crisis or a disaster.

Budgeting and accounting for IT services

Budgeting and accounting for IT services has the goal to budget and account the cost of service provision. Charging is not a direct requirement of the ISO/IEC 20000 Standard. Budgeting and accounting fulfils its tasks in close co-ordination with the company-wide controlling and finance management.

The following policies and procedures should be set up in accordance with the Standard:

- The budgeting and accounting system has to be set up for all components, including IT assets, shared resources, overheads, externally delivered services, personnel, insurance and licences.
- Costs are divided into direct and indirect costs, and are allocated according to the services and cost centres.
- The service provider must implement effective financial control and regulate the authorisation clearly.
- Costs must be planned in appropriate detail, including effective financial control and a basis for decision making.

- Service providers must monitor and manage the budget.
- All changes to the service must be calculated in terms of cost, and authorised by the change management process.

Practical recommendations on the implementation of budgeting and accounting

Budgeting and accounting need not be defined as totally new. Any implementation in this area has to be agreed, and co-ordinated, with the central accounting of the company. It is advisable to create policies for the management of budgeting and accounting processes. These policies have to define the appropriate level of detail, as follows:

- What are the cost elements to be accounted?
- What is the allocation formula for the overhead costs?
- What level of detail of the customer business is to be chosen to notify crediting?
- How to deal with deviation from the budget. Are there any dependencies in terms of size of the deviation? How are deviations escalated to senior management?
- What is the connection to the service level management?

The effort required for the processes of budgeting and accounting must be based on the needs of the customer, service provider and supplier. The benefits of data collection must justify the effort.

The following practical recommendations have to be taken into account for the implementation of the budgeting and accounting process.

Budgeting

The budgeting must take into account any planned changes to services during the budget period and, where necessary, plan to control deficits, so that service levels can be maintained during the year. Budgeting must also take into account any seasonal fluctuations.

The monitoring of costs must provide an early warning system and corresponding procedures for budget variances.

Accounting

The accounting processes monitor the costs in an agreed level of detail and an agreed period of time. All service provider decisions should serve to satisfy the business plans and therefore need this structured financial information.

It is advisable to use cost models that can demonstrate the provision of services. Thus, we get an understanding of the costs, and we are able to assess the impact of reduced service levels, or of a potential loss of service, from a financial point of view.

Capacity management

Capacity management aims to ensure that the service provider always has enough capacity to meet the agreed current and future resource requirements of the business. In this sense, economic viability means that there will be a high utilisation of resources.

To provide sufficient capacity for the storing and processing of data, the capacity management process must ensure the following requirements:

- Capacity management needs to create and update a capacity plan, taking into account the business requirements.
- Methods, procedures and techniques have to be identified and applied, in order to monitor the service capabilities.
- Changes must be examined in terms of their impact for existing capacity.
- Influences of technological developments have to be forecast.
- The capacity plan must create an analysis of the current service capacity, as a basis for decision making for future needs.

Practical recommendations on the implementation of capacity management

With the capacity management resource, bottlenecks should be avoided proactively. To meet the requirements of the capacity management, the following best practice recommendations are made:

The service provider must understand the current and future requirements from the business perspective, and so derive the future IT needs, aligned to the strategic business development.

Derived from the business strategy, the demand forecasts and capacity estimates have to be translated into specific requirements for the IT infrastructure. For this purpose, the load response of the participating service components, under different transaction volumes, has to be technically understood.

The data on current and past-related component and resource utilisation should be collected and analysed for capacity prognosis.

New or changed services have to be assessed with regard to the future capacity needs in the various life stages, and prepared accordingly.

The capacity plan, which documents the current performance of the infrastructure and the anticipated requirements, has to be created and updated at least once a year.

The purpose of all measures in the capacity management is the achievement of the agreed service level targets.

Information security management

Information security management has the goal to control, and to monitor effectively, the information security for all service activities. The Standard refers to the Code of Practice ISO/IEC 27002, which forms a good basis for the implementation of information security.

To meet the requirements of information security management, the following specifications have to be fulfilled:

- Top management has to authorise an information security policy and communicate it to all employees, customers and suppliers.
- Adequate security controls (e.g. virus protection, firewalls, security awareness programmes) have to be used and documented, to enforce the requirements of the security policy.

- The documentation of security controls has to describe the inherent risks, and the nature of the operation and maintenance of controls.
- All arrangements to meet the security requirements must be based on a formal agreement that defines all the necessary security requirements.

Practical recommendations on the implementation of information security management

Information security is a system of guidelines and procedures for identification, control and protection of information, and all equipment related to its storage, transmission and processing. To meet the requirements for information security management, we provide best practice recommendations in the following structure:

- IT security principles
- Identification and classification of information assets
- Security risk assessment
- Controls
- Documents and records.

IT security policies

The service provider uses the IT security policies as a basis for comprehensive security management. With the definition of roles and responsibilities, all employees are sensitised for potential security problems.

The IT security policy also provides information for professional internal audits and serves as a reference point for a variety of secure access controls and secure applications.

The security policies are binding on all members of the company, and when used with appropriate care and sensitivity, can be of great help to the decision-making process of the management. The security policy also applies to external partners and must be agreed by contract.

The requirements for confidentiality, integrity and availability are determined by the classification of IT assets.

The information security policy is mandatory for anyone who is working in, or with, the company (employees, contractors, consultants or suppliers). Their compliance is checked on a regular basis. It is expected that all employees follow this policy and the resulting standards and guidelines.

Risk management is an important building block for the security activities of the service provider. It supports the organisational security measures and helps to optimise internal audits and the documentation. Regulatory compliance is an essential part of the Internal Control System (ICS), which supports the satisfaction of legal and corporate responsibilities needs.

Identification and classification of information assets

Information assets and data must be managed by the configuration management and have to be classified by service criticality. We have to assign, for each service asset, a responsible person for its protection. The daily operations of the information assets can be delegated to internal or external bodies.

Security risk assessment

It is recommended to carry out security risk assessments at agreed intervals. Identified risks should be assessed regarding their impact and likelihood of occurrence, and documented.

When determining the risks, it is advisable to consider the following issues carefully:

- What are the risks in the disclosure of sensitive information to unauthorised parties?
- What are the effects of inaccurate, incomplete or invalid information for the decision process?
- What are the consequences for customers if data and information are suddenly no longer available?
- Are there additional customer-specific, legal or regulatory, security requirements?

Controls

In the context of 'good practice', a service provider should employ measures of control. A control is defined as a guide with procedures, practices and organisational structures. It has to be developed with a sufficient security, so that security goals are achieved, and adverse events prevented, detected and corrected. These controls must be defined for all service management processes during the design, and be considered for implementation in the service design package.

A management team has to be appointed for monitoring and maintaining the effectiveness of the information security policy. Employees with specific security roles are to be trained accordingly.

10: Service Delivery Processes

Documents and records

Security records are to be analysed periodically. The following reports should be handed out at regular intervals to the management of the service provider:

- How effective is the information security policy?
- Are trends in information security incidents determined?
- Is there sufficient control over access to information assets and systems?

With the implementation of a comprehensive information security management system, the foundation for an effective security policy is built. Thus, the basis for trustworthy and reliable services is created.

CHAPTER 11: RELATIONSHIP PROCESSES

The relationship processes describe the two aspects of business relationship management and supplier management. The Standard focuses on the role of the service provider (often the IT organisation of a company), which is logically set between customers and suppliers.

Both customers and suppliers may be within, or outside, the service provider organisation. The contracts are generally distinguished by the following three levels:

- The agreements between the customer and the service providers are called Service Level Agreement (SLAs).
- Necessary external support (suppliers) for the agreed IT services is formalised with Underpinning Contracts (UC).
- Operational Level Agreements (OLA) govern the relations within the IT organisation for service provision.

To achieve good relations between all stakeholders, clear agreements have to be made. Like this, all participants have a common understanding regarding the business requirements, the capacity, the conditions and the respective responsibilities. Then everyone can meet their obligations.

The relationship processes support the ensuring of adequate customer satisfaction. This includes the early understanding of future business requirements and the communication to all parties concerned.

The scope, roles and responsibilities of the business and supplier relationship, must be defined and agreed. Important building blocks for this are the identification of stakeholders, the appropriate means of communication and the appropriate frequency of reports.

Business relationship management

Business relationship management has the aim to understand the customers and the drivers of the business, and to use that knowledge to establish a good relationship between the service provider and the customer.

The specifications of the business relationship management are defined in the following requirements:

- The service provider has to identify all stakeholders and customers of the services, and document them.
- The service provider and the customer shall meet, at least annually, for a service review, to assess changes in service scope, SLAs, contracts, and current and projected business needs.
- At agreed intervals, meetings are carried out to discuss performance, achievements, events and action plans.
- Defined change measures of such meetings are to be placed under the control of the change management process.
- For more significant changes (major changes), the service provider is required to inform its customers continuously, to respond to changing needs.

Practical recommendations on the implementation of business relationship management

To meet the requirements for business relationship management, three important aspects have to be established in the organisation:

- Regular service reviews
- Service complaints
- Measuring customer satisfaction.

Regular service reviews

Service reviews should be carried out at least annually and before and after major service changes. The effective performance in the past period, current and future business needs, as well as proposals to change the scope of the services, should be covered by these reviews.

It makes sense to agree to reviews between major reviews, to address the current status, progress and any problems. The findings of these reviews have to be recorded and reported to the stakeholders. Reached agreements shall be monitored during their implementation.

The service provider must achieve a partnership, rather than a simple relationship, with the customer. This is the only way to ensure that all the business needs and changes are transparent, and all parties are allowed an appropriate response.

Service complaints

It is good practice to agree a process between the customer and the service provider, so that complaints can be dealt with objectively, and responded to appropriately. All service complaints should be documented, promptly investigated, and executed as quickly as possible. Regular reports about the status of the complaint should be made to the customer. Upon successful completion, it is recommended to formally close the complaint, in accordance with the customer.

Unfinished complaints should be monitored regularly. If the complaints are not resolved within the time agreed with the customer, they have to be escalated to the service management.

The service providers should regularly analyse the resulting complaints and identify possible trends. These have to be treated during the regular client meetings and can be used for the implementation of service improvements.

Measuring customer satisfaction

Customer satisfaction should be measured regularly to ensure that the service provider can compare the job performance with the objectives, and with previous surveys. The scope and structure of the surveys must be designed in a way, so that the customer can submit their views with little effort.

If there are significant deviations occurring in customer satisfaction, they must be understood and properly investigated. The results and conclusions should be discussed with the customer. Having an agreed action plan with the customer, is the foundation for the following service improvement initiatives. Customer's compliments should be forwarded to the service delivery team.

Supplier management

Supplier management aims to manage all suppliers, to ensure a smooth provision of a high quality service.

In general, several suppliers are involved. They are often subdivided into principal contractor and sub-contractors with suppliers. It must be clearly established whether the service provider directly negotiates with all suppliers, or whether a major supplier accepts responsibility for subcontracted suppliers. The supplier management process must ensure the following requirements:

- The supplier management process has to be documented. For each supplier, a contract manager has to be appointed.
- The scope of services to be delivered by the supplier (requirements, scope, service levels and communication processes) should be described and formally agreed.
- The supplier agreements have to be agreed with the service level agreements.
- The interfaces between the processes and the involved parties must be documented and agreed.
- All roles and relationships between key suppliers and subcontractors must be documented and communicated.

Practical recommendations on the implementation of supplier management

The supplier management process must ensure that the supplier understands their obligations to the service provider. Therefore, the requirements have to be clearly defined and agreed. It is also essential to ensure that all changes in the agreements are managed by the change management process.

To avoid conflict, it is best to log all official business transactions, between all parties. The performance of suppliers should be monitored continuously. If deviations in the performance or quality of the service of the supplier are detected, an appropriate response must be made.

The following sections describe all of the necessary aspects needed to set up an effective supplier management.

Contract management

The service provider shall appoint a manager who is responsible for all vendor contracts and agreements. It is also recommended that for each supplier, a contact person on the service provider side is assigned.

In addition, a method for monitoring the supplier performance has to be set up. Each supplier contract includes a plan for the regular review of business goals. Moreover, the basis for any contractual bonus or penalties must be declared explicitly. Compliance or violation of this rule shall be documented and reported to the appropriate authorities.

Service definition

The service provider has to define the scope of services for all services of the supplier. The roles and responsibilities, the signature authorisations, and the conditions for the contract termination, have to be determined. Other components of the service definition are the payment and the reporting.

Management of contractual disputes

The service provider and the supplier define in the contract the process for the settlement of contractual disputes. For disputes that cannot be resolved through normal channels, an escalation point needs to be generated. The process also needs to ensure that such disputes are documented, handled appropriately and formally concluded.

Termination of contract

Contract management should include a definition for regular and early contract termination. In order not to risk a unilateral dependence, it is strongly recommended to define the transfer of service from the supplier to a third party as part of any vendor contract.

CHAPTER 12: RESOLUTION PROCESSES

The resolution processes include incident and service request management and problem management. These are separate processes, even if they are closely linked. Incident management deals with the recovery of the service for service users. Secondly, service request management is grouped here to include management of information requests or requests for standard services. Problem management is similar, yet contrasts with incident management, as it focuses on the determination and removal of causes for large or recurrent problems, thus ensuring a sustainable and stable service infrastructure.

Incident and service request management

Incident management has the following objective: to recover the agreed service to the business as quickly as possible and to respond to service requests.

To recover the agreed service as quickly as possible, the necessary procedures have to be defined and followed. In particular, the incident management process has to ensure the following requirements:

- All incidents must be recorded.
- There are methods for controlling the impacts of incidents used.
- Procedures for recording, prioritisation, business impact determination, classification, updating, escalation, resolution and formal closing of all incidents must be defined.

- The customer must always be informed about the status of reported incidents and service request.

- All employees involved in the incident management process need access to all relevant information, such as known errors, solutions and the Configuration Management Database (CMDB).

- Major incidents must be classified as such. A separate process for the solution of these disturbances has to be provided.

The same parameters found within incident management can be applied to service request management. The difference lies in the definition of an incident and a service request – obviously, the scope of a service request is around the management of information requests, providing advice, providing access to services or data or the delivery of a standard change.

Service requests will be defined by the organisation and their fulfilment will follow predefined procedures, priority, and the ability to use relevant and necessary information in order to fulfil the request.

Practical recommendations on the implementation of incident and service request management

To meet the requirements of the specifications, we need to ensure that the incident management is designed both as a reactive, and proactive, process. The process must focus on the restoration of the affected IT services, and not deal with the determination of the cause.

The incident process (incidents and service requests) includes the call-receiving, recording, prioritisation, consideration of security rules, and the tracking of the incident and processing status. Moreover, the degree of fault processing with the client, and any escalation procedure, should be defined.

All incidents must be recorded, so that the relevant information can be identified and analysed. The work progress has to be reported to all affected stakeholders. All activities must be completely recorded in the incident ticket.

Customers must, whenever possible, be able to continue their business properly. This can also be in the form of workarounds.

Major incidents

For the handling of large disturbances which can have a large impact on the business, a separate procedure needs to be set up. It is important that these so-called major incidents are clearly defined and communicated. To eliminate such large problems, we need a pre-designated responsible manager, who is authorised to take all necessary measures (escalations, summoning of external experts) to solve this major incident as quickly as possible.

Problem management

Problem management aims, through proactive identification and analysis of the causes of service incidents, to minimise effects to the business.

Problem management proactively prevents the repetition or recurrence of incidents and known errors. The following specifications must be met:

• All identified problems should be recorded.

- Procedures have to be established to identify, minimise and prevent the impact of incidents and problems.
- Procedures have to be established for recording, classification, updating, escalation, resolution and closing of all problems.
- Preventive measures are to be taken to reduce potential problems, e.g. tracking of trend analysis on incident volumes.
- To address the underlying cause of the problem, amendments have to be passed to the change management process.

Practical recommendations on the implementation of problem management

The problem management needs to identify the underlying causes of incidents and proactively prevent their recurrence. Problems are classified as known errors, once the root cause is known, and present a solution method for avoiding such incidents.

For supplying the incident management well with information, all known errors and the concerned IT services have to be documented, and the associated configuration items identified. Known errors will only be closed after final, successful solution.

After the root cause has been identified, the solution is to be processed via the change management process. Details of the progress, potential workarounds and permanent solutions, are communicated to all stakeholders concerned.

The closing of problem tickets should always be done with the following checks:

- Is the solution documented accurately?

- Is the cause categorised to support further analysis in the future?
- Have affected customers and support staff been informed regarding the solution?
- Has the customer confirmed that they will accept the solution?
- Has the customer been informed if no solution was found?

Finished solutions must be checked regarding their effectiveness. In particular, identify trends, such as recurring problems and incidents, defects, errors, known errors in the planned release, or resource commitments of employees.

Proactive problem management

With proactive measures, the occurrence of incidents and problems can be reduced. The prevention of problems can lead to preventive measures of individual incidents, such as strategic decisions.

The preventive measures in the context of problem management can also include the training of users who can cause incidents, due to lack of knowledge in the management of service.

CHAPTER 13: CONTROL PROCESSES

The control processes create essential conditions for a stable and secure IT operation, through sound management of the IT inventory and ensuring orderly change in IT. Three processes are included: change management, configuration management and release and deployment management.

While change management focuses on the control and co-ordination of changes, release and deployment management prepares the planned changes for their deployment. Configuration management provides the necessary information to not only assess change impact, but also control the information about the components affected by the change. Release and deployment management has to be integrated into the configuration and change management processes, to ensure that the releases and executed changes are co-ordinated. The result of these three processes is a co-ordinated change that has minimal impact on the business operations: it is under control and risk mitigated.

Configuration management

The goal of configuration management is to define the components of the services and infrastructure, and to manage and administer their accurate information.

The configuration management process must ensure the following:

- There must be an integrated approach to change and configuration management.

- Configuration management must have an interface to the financial accounting.
- Configuration Items (CI), associated components and relationships, must be defined.
- The information used for each CI has to be defined.
- Configuration management provides the mechanisms to identify, control and track versions of the components of the infrastructure.

Practical recommendations on the implementation of configuration management

All major assets and configurations should be assigned to a responsible manager, who ensures adequate security and control. This will ensure that, prior to the implementation of changes to the CI, permission has been given.

To meet the specifications of the configuration management process, the following recommendations have been established:

- Planning and implementation
- Configuration identification
- Configuration control
- Status accounting
- Verification and audit.

Planning and implementation

When planning for the implementation of configuration management, an integrated approach with the change and release management should be considered.

The configuration plan should include the following:

- Scope, objectives, principles, standards, roles and responsibilities.
- Description of the processes for the definition and changes to the CIs in service and infrastructure, for the monitoring of changes to the configurations, for the recording and reporting of changes in CI status, and for the verification of the records.
- Requirements of accountability, traceability and auditability.
- Configuration control (access, protection, version).
- Interfaces to the control processes between participating organisations (suppliers, customers).
- Planning and development of resources to bring the assets under control and maintain the configuration management system.
- Management of the suppliers that perform configuration management.

Configuration identification and CMDB

Appropriate relationships and dependencies between CIs should be established, to secure the necessary degree of control. It is the responsibility of the service organisation to ensure the traceability of the entire CI life cycle. CIs should be recorded in the Configuration Management Database (CMDB), together with the following information:

- Information on information systems and software, and related documentation (e.g. specifications, design, reviews, etc.)
- Configuration baselines or building descriptions per environment
- Master hard copies and electronic libraries (e.g. DML: Definitive Media Library)

- Configuration management tools or packages
- Licences
- Security components, e.g. Firewalls
- Physical assets, which must be tracked from asset management.
- Service related documents, e.g. SLAs, procedures
- Service supporting facilities, e.g. power supply
- Relationships and dependencies between CIs.

Configuration control

Configuration control ensures that proposed changes to configuration items are fully coordinated and documented. Configuration management has to ensure that only identified and authorised CIs will be accepted and recorded. Without adequate documentation and control, CIs may not be added, modified or withdrawn.

To protect the integrity of systems, services and infrastructure, CIs are kept in a suitable and safe environment. They have to be protected from unauthorised access, modification or alteration. The possibility for disaster recovery must be taken into account, as well as the controlled removal of a copy of the secured original software.

Configuration status accounting

In order to reflect changes (status, location and version) of CIs, up-to-date and accurate configuration records should be kept. Configuration management reports should be available to all parties. The status accounting must provide current and historical data over the entire life cycle of the CIs.

Configuration verification and audit

Scheduled inspection and audit processes ensure that adequate processes and resources are in place to provide the protection of the physical configurations and the intellectual capital of the organisation. Moreover, it also guarantees that the service provider has its configuration, master copies and licences under control.

Every three to six months, a configuration audit must be executed, to ensure that the physical CIs correspond with their product specifications in the CMDB.

Change management

The objective of change management is to ensure that all changes are assessed with structured methods, and are approved, implemented and verified. The focus here is on timely, cost-effective implementation, with minimal risks for operations.

Changes, such as new releases, version updates, hardware changes, or changes initiated by the incident and problem management, always affect the service environment. To ensure that all modifications are approved, implemented and reviewed, the change management process controls all the changes in the system landscape, with the following specifications:

- The level of service and infrastructure changes is clearly defined and documented.
- All Requests for Change (RFC) are recorded and classified.
- The change management process has to provide solutions in case of failure, so that a change can be reversed by a rollback procedure.

- Changes have to be accepted first and then tested. Afterwards, they are implemented in a controlled manner and introduced in a production environment.
- All changes are reviewed after their implementation. Necessary measures for improvement are identified and initiated.
- For the controlled authorisation and implementation of emergency changes, its own principles and procedures have to be established.

Practical recommendations on the implementation of change management

The change management processes and procedures have to ensure that changes have a clearly defined and documented scope. Only changes with an identified business benefit are authorised. Changes should be planned depending on the priority and the potential risk. Changes to infrastructure components should be verified technically and qualitatively during the change implementation.

The status of the changes, and the planned implementation dates, are the basis for change and release planning. Information regarding dates should be communicated to all stakeholders concerned by the change.

Close and review of change requests

All changes must be reviewed after implementation success or failure. Any improvement measures will be identified and implemented.

After all major changes, a special review, a Post Implementation Review (PIR), should be executed. Here, checks are made as to whether the change reached the goal, the customers are satisfied with the results, and that there were no unexpected side effects.

Emergency changes

Emergency changes must follow the change process as far as possible. Certain aspects can be documented after their implementation. If the emergency change process bypasses other change management requirements, the change must be brought back into conformity with those requirements, as soon as possible afterwards.

Emergency changes must be justified by the implementer and tested accordingly after the change. Evidence has to be supplied that it actually is an emergency.

Release management

Release management aims to deliver one or more changes in a release into the production environment and to track it.

Optimal planning and structured management are critical for a successful deployment of a release and the necessary accompanying measures:

- The release management process must be integrated with the configuration and change management process operations.
- Release principles must be defined, which determine the frequency and type of release. These are documented and agreed with the customer.
- The service provider plans the release of the services, systems, software and hardware, co-ordinating with the

business. Rollout plans of releases shall be agreed by all relevant parties.
* The process also provides for rollback scenarios.

Practical recommendations on the implementation of release management

A major task of the release management process is the co-ordination of all resources in order to deploy a release in a distributed environment. Good planning and good management are essential to create releases, to successfully distribute, and to have the associated risks to the business and IT under control.

It is advisable to plan in advance all aspects of the release, together with the business. That means that all the effects on all associated CIs must be evaluated, and both the technical and non-technical aspects must be considered together.

All release elements must be able to be traced back and protected against change. Only tested and approved releases may be accepted in the production environment.

Release policy

The release policy should cover at least the following aspects:

* Frequency and nature of the release
* Roles and responsibilities in release management
* Decision-making body for the transfer to the acceptance test and into the production environment
* Clear identification and description of the releases
* Approach to bundling of changes to a release

- Approach to automation for the construction of the release, distribution and installation
- Verification and acceptance.

Release and rollout planning

The deployment is finally the real task and goal of the release management process. In order to avoid negative surprises, the rollout has to be planned accordingly. The service provider must ensure with the business that the CIs of a release are compatible with the target environment. The release plan ensures that the changes to the affected systems and services are agreed, authorised, planned, co-ordinated and pursued.

The following aspects should be considered:

- Release date and description of the related work
- Associated changes, problems, known errors and new known errors found during testing
- Associated processes
- Back-out procedures
- Acceptance process
- Communication
- Documentation
- Training of the customer
- Logistics and processes for purchasing, storage, disposal, etc.
- Necessary support resources
- Identification of the dependencies and associated risks
- Release sign-off
- Planning of possible audits.

13: Control Processes

Design, build and configuration of a release

Upon receipt, the systems and releases created by the in-house or external development teams will be reviewed by release management, and documented by the configuration management. The release and distribution should be designed to achieve the following goals and implement:

- Conformity to the standards of the service provider
- Integrity during all phases
- Use of authorised libraries
- Identification of risks and implementation of response measures
- Verification of the target platform before the release
- Verification that a release is complete after the transfer.

The output of the build process provides us with release notes, installation instructions and installed software, and hardware associated with a configuration baseline. These outputs are passed to the test group to examine their function in detail. To increase effectiveness and efficiency, these phases should be automated as much as possible.

Release verification and acceptance

Each release must receive a formal sign-off by authorised personnel. The process of verification and acceptance should include:

- Verification that the test environment corresponds to the production environment
- Assurance that the release is built from controlled CIs
- Verification of the execution of appropriate testing
- Assurance that the tests were conducted to the satisfaction of the business and IT

- Assurance that the release authority signs each stage of the acceptance tests
- Verification, before the installation, that the target platform meets the hardware and software requirements
- Verification that a release is complete after deployment.

Documentation

The recommendation is to provide adequate documentation and to put it under the control of configuration management. The documentation should include:

- Full support documentation
- System overview, and installation and support procedures
- Build, release, installation and deployment processes
- Emergency and back-out plans
- Training plans for IT and the business
- Configuration baseline with the associated CIs
- Associated changes, problems and known errors
- Detection of the release authorisation
- Verification and acceptance
- Details of known errors are to be communicated to the incident management
- If the release is rejected, delayed or cancelled, the change management has to be informed.

Rollout, deployment and installation

The rollout plan must be reviewed in advance. It must be ensured that the release can be safely deployed to its destination platform. The rollout, deployment and installation processes ensure that:

- All hardware and software storage areas are safe
- Appropriate procedures for storage, delivery, reception and disposal exist
- Checks on installations, equipment and electrical systems are planned and conducted
- All stakeholders are aware of new releases
- Unnecessary products, services and licences are disabled.

Releases should be checked for usability and completeness. After successful installation, all CIs have to be updated with location and owner. The results of customer acceptance and satisfaction surveys have to be handed over to the business relationship management.

After rollout, deployment and installation

Incidents which can be assigned to releases have to be measured and analysed after the implementation. The change management process performs a Post Implementation Review (PIR). Recommendations from the review should be included in the Service Improvement Plan (SIP).

CHAPTER 14: PREPARING FOR THE AUDIT

As the very latest stage in the preparation for the certification audit, the final scope of the audit should be defined with the auditor, in order to outline the framework for the upcoming certification. The IT service manager must also monitor the readiness of the IT service organisation, clean up the documents for the certification audit, and compile them in a dossier for the auditor. Finally, the exact timing and resources required for the certification audit must be agreed with the certification company.

The certification audit is an essential indicator of the situation of the management system.

Drawing on the Standard ISO/IEC 20000 itself, as well as the document designed for the implementation of the management system (implementation plan for IT service management), the degree of compliance from the evidence or documentary records generated, has to be evaluated.

Non-conformities, the actions of improvements identified in certification audit, and the proposed corrective action plan to overcome them, are essential to the phase of the management review.

The certification audit is usually presented as a heavyweight document audit. For this reason, it is important that the documentation can be presented to the auditor clearly structured. The auditor gets, on the basis of these documents, their first impression of the quality and the ISO/IEC 20000 maturity of the IT service organisation. The document management framework and process management system will be proved here for the first time.

After reviewing the documents and interviewing some of the process managers, the certification auditor creates a report about the certification audit. In this report, the individual processes are assessed in general and suggestions for their improvement are made in view of the certification audit. Based on this report, a certification body will award the ISO/IEC 20000 certificate and license the use of any related logo to the service provider.

Do not confuse the certification audit with the internal audit as described in the Standard. The internal audit is performed by the service provider at various intervals to ensure the SMS and the processes are compliant to the requirements. These internal audits are in addition to the formal certification and annual surveillance audits by the certification body.

Good audit procedures should be deployed in the internal audit, such as independence – process owners should not audit their own process. The internal audit should not be influenced by organisational politics, but, rather, Standard requirements. These audits can follow various schedules (e.g. staggered to minimise disruption), as long as they are planned, there is no requirement that internal audits must mirror the certification or surveillance audit.

Lastly, the benefits of fulfilling the requirements can still be achieved without completing the formal certification audit. Organisations should deploy the areas where they will gain the most value for their resources spent. Of course, it is a bit 'easier' to comply to process requirements when an external organisation will be assessing and reporting their findings.

APPENDIX A: BIBLIOGRAPHY

- ISO/IEC 20000-1:2011 Information technology – Service management – Part 1: Service management system requirements.
- ISO/IEC 20000-2:2012 Information technology – Service management – Part 2: Guidance on the application of service management systems.
- ISO/IEC 20000-3:2012 Information technology – Service management – Part 3: Guidance on scope definition and applicability of ISO/IEC 20000-1.
- ISO/IEC TR 20000-4:2010 Information technology – Service management – Part 4: Process reference model.
- ISO/IEC TR 20000-5:2010 Information technology – Service management – Part 5: Exemplar implementation plan for ISO/IEC 20000-1.
- BrightTALK webcast: Destination ISO/IEC 20000: Industry News and Updates webcast, Channel:itSMF USA, 17 Feb 2011.
- Network Centric Solutions-2 (NETCENTS-2) Enterprise Integration and Service Management Draft Request for Proposal (RFP), FA8771-09-R-0008.

ITG RESOURCES

IT Governance Ltd. sources, creates and delivers products and services to meet the real-world, evolving IT governance needs of today's organisations, directors, managers and practitioners.

The ITG website (*www.itgovernance.co.uk*) is the international one-stop-shop for corporate and IT governance information, advice, guidance, books, tools, training and consultancy.

http://www.itgovernance.co.uk/itil.aspx is the information page on our website for ITIL resources.

Other Websites

Books and tools published by IT Governance Publishing (ITGP) are available from all business booksellers and are also immediately available from the following websites:

http://www.itgovernance.eu is our euro-denominated website which ships from Benelux and has a growing range of books in European languages other than English.

www.itgovernanceusa.com is a US dollar-based website that delivers the full range of IT Governance products to North America, and ships from within the continental US.

www.itgovernanceasia.com provides a selected range of ITGP products specifically for customers in the Indian sub-continent.

www.itgovernance.asia delivers the full range of ITGP publications, serving countries across Asia Pacific and shipping from Hong Kong. US dollars, Singapore dollars, Hong Kong dollars, New Zealand dollars and Thai baht are all accepted through the website.

www.27001.com is the IT Governance Ltd. website that deals specifically with information security management, and ships from within the continental US.

Toolkits

ITG's unique range of toolkits includes the IT Governance Framework Toolkit, which contains all the tools and guidance that you will need in order to develop and implement an appropriate IT governance framework for your organisation. Full details can be found at *www.itgovernance.co.uk/ products/519*.

For a free paper on how to use the proprietary Calder-Moir IT Governance Framework, and for a free trial version of the toolkit, see *www.itgovernance.co.uk/calder_moir.aspx*.

There is also a wide range of toolkits to simplify implementation of management systems, such as an ISO/IEC 27001 ISMS or an ISO/IEC 22301 BCMS, and these can all be viewed and purchased online at: *http://www.itgovernance.co.uk/catalog/1*.

Training Services

IT Governance offers an extensive portfolio of training courses designed to educate information security, IT governance, risk management and compliance professionals. Our classroom and online training programmes will help you develop the skills required to deliver best practice and compliance to your organisation. They will also enhance your career by providing you with industry-standard certifications and increased peer recognition. Our range of courses offer a structured learning path from foundation to advanced level in the key topics of information security, IT governance, business continuity and service management.

ISO/IEC 20000 is the first international standard for IT service management and has been developed to reflect the best practice guidance contained within the ITIL framework. Our ISO20000 Foundation and Practitioner training courses are designed to provide delegates with a comprehensive introduction and guide to the implementation of an ISO20000 management system and an industry-recognised qualification awarded by APMG International.

Full details of all IT Governance training courses can be found at *http://www.itgovernance.co.uk/training.aspx*.

Professional Services and Consultancy

As IT Service Management becomes ever more important in organisations of all sizes and levels of business complexity, so the deployment of best practice (e.g. ITIL), and the development of a management system that can be certified to ISO/IEC 20000, becomes a greater challenge for the lead implementers. This is especially true when management systems that were set up and managed separately have to be integrated to achieve the most cost-effective and efficient corporate structure.

Our consultants can transfer the knowledge that you need to implement ISO20000, bringing IT service management considerations in line with other systems, such as ISO/IEC 27001, ISO22301, ISO14001, and COBIT®. By adopting a standards-based approach, you will be able to clearly show your clients that you offer the highest quality in your services.

We can also help you to support continuing improvements by measuring whether your IT services are adding real value to your business, more than justifying the cost of implementation.

For more information about IT Governance Consultancy for IT Service Management, see: *http://www.itgovernance.co.uk/itsm-itil-iso20000-consultancy.aspx*.

Publishing Services

IT Governance Publishing (ITGP) is the world's leading IT-GRC publishing imprint that is wholly owned by IT Governance Ltd.

With books and tools covering all IT governance, risk and compliance frameworks, we are the publisher of choice for authors and distributors alike, producing unique and practical publications of the highest quality, in the latest formats available, which readers will find invaluable.

www.itgovernancepublishing.co.uk is the website dedicated to ITGP, enabling both current and future authors, distributors, readers and other interested parties, to have easier access to more information allowing them to keep up to date with the latest publications and news from ITGP.

Newsletter

IT governance is one of the hottest topics in business today, not least because it is also the fastest moving.

You can stay up-to-date with the latest developments across the whole spectrum of IT governance subject matter, including risk management, information security, ITIL and IT service management, project governance, compliance and so much more, by subscribing to ITG's core publications and topic alert emails.

Simply visit our subscription centre and select your preferences: *www.itgovernance.co.uk/newsletter.aspx*.